This Notebook Belongs To

Made in the USA
Las Vegas, NV
03 September 2022

54619118R00068